Rain Forests

by Shirley W. Gray

Content Adviser: Terrence E. Young Jr., M.Ed., M.L.S.,
Jefferson Parish (La.) Public Schools

Reading Adviser: Dr. Linda D. Labbo,
Department of Reading Education, College of Education,
The University of Georgia

COMPASS POINT BOOKS

Minneapolis, Minnesota

Compass Point Books
3109 West 50th Street, #115
Minneapolis, MN 55410

Visit Compass Point Books on the Internet at *www.compasspointbooks.com* or e-mail your
request to *custserv@compasspointbooks.com*

Photographs ©:
Dave Watts/Tom Stack and Associates, cover; Visuals Unlimited/D. Cavagnaro, 4; James P. Rowan, 5; Photo Network/Grace Davies, 6;
Photo Network/Mark Newman, 7; FPG/Toyohiro Yamada, 8; Visuals Unlimited/Joe McDonald, 9; James P. Rowan, 10; FPG/Telegraph
Colour Library, 11; Visuals Unlimited/Bayard H. Brattstrom, 12; Root Resources/Kitty Kohart, 14; FPG/Charles Benes, 15; Tom Stack &
Associates/John Shaw, 16; Photo Network/Chad Ehlers, 18; International Stock/Chad Ehlers, 19; International Stock/George Ancona, 20;
Root Resources/Byron Crader, 21; Visuals Unlimited/Inga Spence, 22; Visuals Unlimited/John D. Cunningham, 23; FPG/Dennis Cody,
24; Photo Network/Chad Ehlers, 25; Photo Network/William Mitchell, 26; Tom Stack & Associates/Joe McDonald, 27; Tom Stack &
Associates/Robert Fried, 28; Tom Stack & Associates/W. Perry Conway, 29; Tom Stack & Associates/Brian Parker, 30; Visuals
Unlimited/Vul G. Prance, 31; Michael Fogden/Bruce Coleman Inc., 32; Tom Stack & Associates/W. Perry Conway, 33; James P. Rowan,
34; Visuals Unlimited/Ken Lucas, 35; James P. Rowan, 36, 37; Visuals Unlimited/Vul G. Prance, 38; International Stock/Chad Ehlers, 39;
Visuals Unlimited/Thomas Gula, 40; FPG/Gail Shumway, 41; Tom Stack & Associates/W. Perry Conway, 42; Photo Network/Grace
Davies, 43.

Editors: E. Russell Primm and Emily J. Dolbear
Photo Researcher: Svetlana Zhurkina
Photo Selector: Dawn Friedman
Design: Bradfordesign, Inc.
Cartography: XNR Productions, Inc.

Library of Congress Cataloging-in-Publication Data

Gray, Shirley W.
    Rain forests / by Shirley W. Gray.
        p. cm. — (First reports)
    Includes bibliographical references (p.   ) and index.
    Summary: Describes what a rain forest is and what types of plants and animals reside there.
    ISBN 0-7565-0023-0 (hardcover : lib. bdg.)
    ISBN 0-7565-0949-1 (paperback)
        1. Rain forest ecology—Juvenile literature. 2. Rain forests—Juvenile literature. [1. Rain forest
ecology. 2. Ecology. 3. Rain forests.] I. Title. II. Series.
    QH541.5.R27 G72 2000
    577.34—dc21   00-008534

Table of Contents

What Can You Imagine? 4

Tropical Rain Forests 7

Temperate Rain Forest 14

Trees in the Rain Forests 18

Layers of Life 22

Animals and Life Cycles 26

Hanging, Swinging Animals 31

Creeping, Crawling Animals 35

Who Lives in the Rain Forest? 37

The Importance of Rain Forests 39

Protecting the Rain Forests 43

Glossary 44

Did You Know? 45

At a Glance 46

Want to Know More? 47

Index 48

What Can You Imagine?

▲ *A colorful tropical plant*

Imagine a spider that can eat a bird or a snake that can fly. Imagine a flower that grows without soil or a fish that eats fruit. These unusual plants and animals are not from someone's imagination. They are real—they live in tropical rain forests.

Millions of other strange and interesting plants and animals live in the rain forests. Of all the kinds, or **species**, of plants on Earth, more than half live there. Scientists are still discovering new insects in the forest.

Many of the animals of the rain forests do not live anywhere else on Earth. The maues marmoset is a new species of monkey in the Amazon rain forests in South America. It is so small, it can fit in the palm of a person's hand.

▲ *Many animals, such as poison dart frogs, live in the world's rain forests.*

▲ *A mountainous tropical rain forest.*

Tropical Rain Forests

Tropical rain forests grow near the **equator**. The equator is the belt of Earth where the air is always warm. The temperatures are usually around 79° Fahrenheit (26° Celsius).

Because it's warm, the trees stay green year-round and do not lose their leaves. Many birds such as parrots and macaws live there all the time.

▲ *A hyacinth macaw*

Rain is important in these forests. Tropical rain

forests in Latin America receive as much as about 1,000 inches (2,540 centimeters) of rain every year. The leaves of the trees are so big and thick that the rain does not fall straight to the ground. Instead, the water pools on the leaves or runs down the trunks of the trees. Below the leafy branches, the air feels warm and wet.

▲ *These climbing plants called lianas can be found in Costa Rica.*

In the middle of the rain forests, the tree trunks are smooth and straight. Climbing plants called lianas hang from the trees. These woody vines may grow to be as thick as a man's arm.

▲ *This orchid grows in the rain forests of Malaysia.*

Tropical flowers called orchids and bromeliads often grow on the branches and tree trunks. They do not need soil. Instead, their roots absorb food from the air and rainwater.

The largest tropical rain forest is in South America.

▲ *The Amazon River*

It grows along the Amazon River across Brazil, Peru, and other countries. Other large tropical forests grow in the **lowlands** of the Congo River in Africa. Smaller rain forests grow in Australia and Mexico.

Some tropical rain forests grow in the **highlands**.

▲ Misty clouds cover the Andes Mountains in Peru.

Because they are higher up, these rain forests may be cooler than forests in the lowlands. The trees are usually shorter. Ferns and bamboos are common.

These rain forests are sometimes called cloud forests because misty clouds cover them. They grow in Central Africa, Indonesia, and the Andes Mountains in South America.

Temperate Rain Forests

▲ *Glacier Bay rain forest in Alaska*

Another type of rain forest grows on the northwest
coast of North America. It is called a temperate rain
forest. In temperate rain forests, the rainfall and
dampness in the air, or **humidity**, is high. The winters
are mild. The plant life in a temperate rain forest is
usually not as thick as a tropical forest.

▲ *A rain forest stream in Washington's Mount Rainier*

▲ *An Alaskan brown bear catches a salmon.*

Temperate rain forests are also found in the United States and Canada. Several kinds of bears, bald eagles, wolves, and salmon live in the temperate rain forests in Alaska. Other important rain forests are located in the Pacific Northwest of the United States and southwestern Canada.

Trees in the Rain Forest

▲ *Tree roots are close to the surface to absorb as much water as possible.*

In the rain forest, trees grow 200 to 265 feet (61 to 81 meters) high. But their roots are close to the surface of the soil. These roots soak up water that falls to the ground. They also help the trees absorb food from the dead plants and animals that rot on the forest floor.

▲ Gum trees are common in rain forests.

▲ *Bamboo is one of the many useful products from the rain forest.*

▲ *A cocoa tree with ripe pods*

Many trees grow in the rain forests. In one tropical forest in Malaysia, scientists counted almost 8,000 species of trees. Many of the trees produce fruit, nuts, and seeds, such as the cocoa tree.

Layers of Life

▲ *A view from the tops of the rain forest trees*

Rain forests grow in layers. The tops, or crowns, of the tallest trees create what is called the **emergent layer**. Here the trees are separated by wide spaces. The top branches get plenty of sunlight and rain.

Under the emergent layer is the **canopy**. This

▲ *The canopy of a tropical rain forest*

section is made of shorter trees that may only grow
to about 165 feet (50 meters). This is the thickest part
of the forest because it is crowded. Little sunlight gets
through the thick blanket of leaves and branches.
Some rain forests have more than one layer of
canopy.

▲ *Thick leaf cover allows very little sunlight to the rain forest's lower layers.*

Under the canopy is the **understory**. The understory is the layer of trees and shrubs between the canopy and the forest floor. Very little sunlight reaches the young trees and shrubs here.

At the bottom is the **forest floor**. All that grows in the dark shade are new tree sprouts and small green plants. In many rain forests, the floor is almost bare. Leaves that fall to the ground rot quickly because of the warmth and dampness.

▲ *Fir and hemlock trees shade the forest floor in Washington's Mount Rainier National Park.*

Animals and Life Cycles

▲ *The thick forest covering provides a safe home to millions of unseen animals.*

The tropical rain forests are alive with animals. Many of them have changed to survive in the forests. For example, birds hide under the canopy's thick leaves to escape the tarantula, a spider that feeds on young or injured birds.

▲ *A leaf-nosed bat flies through a tropical rain forest.*

Many kinds of bats live in rain forests around the world. A large supply of insects satisfies the large appetites of these bats.

▲ *A keel-billed toucan*

Some birds of the forests have long narrow beaks that help them dig insects out of tree limbs. Parrots and toucans are birds with large, strong beaks. They use their beaks to open nuts like nutcrackers.

▲ *Scarlet macaws eat clay to calm upset stomachs in addition to fruit and seeds.*

Birds and other animals that eat fruit help the **life cycle** of the rain forests. They may carry the seed of one fruit to another part of the forest and drop it. Then a new tree grows.

▲ *A pirarucu swims in the Amazon River.*

In the Amazon River, fish help the life cycle of the trees. The pirarucu is one of the largest freshwater fish in the world. It can jump out of the water to snag fruit hanging over the river. The fish eats the fruit, and the river carries the seeds to another area of the forest.

Hanging, Swinging Animals

Animals that live in trees are called **arboreal**. Arboreal animals have developed special features to help them live in trees.

For example, the three-toed sloth, one of which is called the ai, has long and well-developed limbs.

These animals have a long, curved claws at the end of their limbs. Claws such as these help the sloth hang from branches high above the rain forest floor. Three-toed sloths may come down to the ground as little as once a week.

▲ *A three-toed sloth*

The banded anteater uses its tail to move from one tree branch to another. Other rain forest animals have developed special tails to survive. Banded anteaters, also known as numbats, eat ants and termites with their long, sticky tongues. A numbat has to eat nearly 15,000 termites a day.

▲ *A female orangutan and her baby*

Monkeys also use their tails to help them swing from tree to tree as they search for food. Orangutans can travel for miles in the rain forests using the limbs of the canopy as a highway.

▲ *A tree boa slithers on a branch in Peru.*

Many rain forest animals fly or slither between the tree branches. In the rain forests of Borneo, more than thirty species of animals glide from tree to tree.

Creeping, Crawling Animals

Some large animals live on the rain forest floor. The tapir is a shy animal that looks like a pig with a long snout. Even though tapirs are big—heavier than a gorilla—it is hard to see one in the forest.

▲ *The Malayan tapir is an endangered species.*

In fact, most of the animals living on the forest floor are hidden. Thousands of insects, such as ants, beetles, and termites, crawl unseen.

Armies of leaf-cutter ants march quietly from their mounds in the ground to the tops of the trees. Then, they slice the leaves into small pieces and carry them back to the mounds. When leaf-cutter ants are at work, the forest floor is alive with moving green leaves.

Who Lives in the Rain Forest?

Plants and animals are not the only living things that have changed to survive in the rain forests. Many groups of people have lived in the rain forests for thousands of years. In Brazil, native people still hunt and fish along the Amazon River.

▲ *A village along the Amazon River*

▲ *A boy living in the Amazon River basin*

The people who live along the Congo River in central Africa hunt meat and gather honey in the rain forests. Adults are usually shorter than 5 feet (1.5 meters), but they are very strong. Their size helps them move easily through the rain forest.

The Importance of Rain Forests

At one time, many people thought the soil of rain forests would be good for farming. So they cut the trees and sold the wood. Then they tried to plant crops. But most rain forest soil is made of clay and is not good for crops. Now people are learning the importance of rain forests.

▲ *Huge parts of Brazil's rain forests have been destroyed.*

▲ *When trees in the rain forests are cut down, the animals have no place to live.*

When trees in a rain forest are cut, sunlight reaches the ground. When this happens, new species of green plants begin crowding the forest floor. The sunlight also warms the inside of the forest and dries up the water.

Cutting trees mean smaller animals have fewer leaves and branches to protect them from enemies. They also have fewer places to live and trouble finding food.

Large animals such as leopards and jaguars need miles and miles of rain forest land. This is so they have enough room to hunt. Large apes have to travel for miles to find fruit to eat. Small rain forests would mean these animals would not have enough food to live.

▲ A jaguar in the wild

▲ *Rain forest seed pods and fruits may contain cures for human diseases.*

Thousands of animal species have already died out because people have cut down their trees. Many plant species depend on animals to scatter their seeds and pollen. Some kinds of plants have died out too.

Some animals and plants of the rain forests contain natural chemicals that help people. Scientists use some of these chemicals to make drugs to treat cancer or heart disease.

Protecting the Rain Forests

Many people are now working to protect the rain forests. The government of Brazil does not allow anyone to cut rain forests trees to sell to other countries. They watch the rain forests with satellites to make sure no one breaks the law.

Imagine life without cocoa and chocolate or Brazilian nuts and cashews. Imagine no cinnamon, vanilla, cloves, or coconut. These foods were first found in the rain forests. Imagine the world without cheetahs, jaguars, or orangutans, without parrots, toucans, or macaws. These animals call the rain forest home—and count on people to keep it alive.

Glossary

arboreal—living in trees

canopy—the layer of the rain forest between the emergent layer and the understory where the growth is thick and there is little sunlight

emergent layer—the top layer of the rain forest where the growth is sparse and there is sunlight

equator—the belt of earth where the air is always warm

forest floor—the bottom layer of the rain forest where there is almost no sunlight

highlands—high or hilly lands

humidity—dampness in the air

life cycle—the series of stages through which a growing thing passes

lowlands—lands that are low compared to the land around it

species—kind

understory—the layer of the rain forest between the canopy and the forest floor where there is very little sunlight

Did You Know?

- Rain forests have more plant and animal species than almost any other habitat in the world.

- Almost 90 percent of the rain forest animal species are insects.

- Although rain forests are green and seem fertile, the soil is really quite poor.

- Rain forests exist as far north as British Columbia in Canada.

- The Amazon River basin covers more than 2.5 million square miles (6.5 million square kilometers).

- Scientists use hot air balloons, cables, towers, and even robots to study the millions of plants and animals in the trees of the rain forest.

At a Glance

Location: Parts of South America, Central America, Asia, Australia, and Africa (tropical rain forest) Pacific Northwest of the United States and southwestern Canada (temperate rain forest)

Amount of rain or snow each year: 100 inches (250 centimeters) (tropical rain forest) Varies (temperate rain forest)

Description: Very wet; temperature stays about the same all year long (tropical rain forest) Mild winters; plant life less thick than in a tropical forest (temperate rain forest)

Common animals: Jaguars, sloths, monkeys, tapirs, parrots (tropical rain forest) Wolves, bears, deer, salmon (temperate rain forest)

Common plants: Lianas, palms, tree ferns, orchids, bromeliads (tropical rain forest) Western hemlock, Douglas fir, mosses, vine maple, ferns (temperate rain forest)

At the Library

Grupper, Jonathan. *Destination: Rain Forest.* Washington, D.C.:
National Geographic Society 1997.

Morgan, Sally. *Saving the Rainforests.* Danbury, Conn.: Franklin Watts,
1999.

Pirotta, Saviour. *Trees and Plants in the Rain Forest.* Austin, Tex.:
Raintree Steck-Vaughn, 1999.

On the Web

For more information on *rain forests*, use FactHound
to track down Web sites related to this book.

1. Go to *www.facthound.com*
2. Type in a search word related to this
   book or this book ID: 0756500230.
3. Click on the *Fetch It* button.

Your trusty FactHound will fetch the best Web sites for you!

Through the Mail

U.S. Environmental Protection Agency
National Service Center for Environmental Publications
P.O. Box 42419
Cincinnati, OH 45242-2419
For free EPA publications about the rain forest

On the Road

Olympic National Forest
1835 Black Lake Boulevard, S.W.
Olympia, WA 98512-5623
To visit a termperate rain forest

Index

Africa, 11, 13
Amazon River, 11, 30, 37
Andes Mountains, 13
animals, 4, 17, 18, 26, 27, 29, 31,
    35, 37, 41, 42
banded anteaters, 32
birds, 4, 7, 17, 26, 28, 29
Brazil, 11, 37
canopies, 22, 23, 24, 26
cloud forests, 13
Congo River, 11, 38
emergent layer, 22
equator, 7
fish, 4, 17, 30
flowers, 10
forest floor, 25
highlands, 11, 12
insects, 5, 26, 27, 35
lowlands, 11, 13

Malaysia, 21
monkeys, 5, 33
North America, 14
parrots, 28
pirarucu, 30
plants, 4, 9, 14, 18, 37, 42
protecting, 43
rain, 7–8, 22
reptiles, 4, 34
roots, 18
soil, 4, 10, 18, 39
South America, 5, 10–11, 13
sunlight, 22, 23, 24
temperatures, 7
three-toed sloth, 31
trees, 8–9, 18, 21, 23, 24, 29
toucans, 28
understories, 24

About the Author

Shirley W. Gray received her bachelor's degree in
education from the University of Mississippi and her
master's degree in technical writing from the University
of Arkansas. She teaches writing and works as a scien-
tific writer and editor. Shirley W. Gray lives with her
husband and two sons in Little Rock, Arkansas.